YOUR DESTINY HAS A DIET

SHIRLEY MCCONICO

Limits of Liability and Disclaimer of Warranty

The author and publisher shall not be liable for your misuse of this material. This book is strictly for informational and educational purposes. The purpose of this book is to educate and entertain. The author and/or publisher do not guarantee that anyone following these techniques, suggestions, tips, ideas, or strategies will become successful. The author and/or publisher shall have neither liability nor responsibility to anyone with respect to any loss or damage caused, or alleged to be caused, directly or indirectly by the information contained in this book. Views expressed in this publication do not necessarily reflect the views of the publisher.

Cover Design: Studio 5 Agency
Printed in the United States of America
ISBN 978-1-948270-26-7
Keen Vision Publishing, LLC
www.keen-vision.com

For my readers,
May you find the nourishment you need to fulfill your destiny.

CONTENTS

INTRODUCTION

"Beloved, I pray that in all things thou mayest prosper and be in health, even as thy soul prospereth."

3 John 1:2 (ASV)

The word *diet* is defined as our daily consumption of food. However, many overlook that we have a natural and spiritual diet we must satisfy daily. In the Greek, diet is *diait*, which means *a way of life*. In Hebrew it's *di-it*. The book of Genesis speaks of a diet of fruits, grains, nuts, and legumes. God wants us to have holistic (holy) health, meaning He wants us to consider the mind, body, and spirit (spiritually whole). For if one part is unhealthy, the entire body is thrown off.

THE BODY

"Or know ye not that your body is [a]temple of the Holy Spirit which is in you, which ye have from God? and ye are not your own;"

1 Corinthians 6:19 (ASV)

Your body is a machine that is constantly repairing, rebuilding, and regenerating cells. The raw materials for these processes come from what we eat. We are what we eat. We must be careful to only consume things that will lead to a healthier life. Our bodies are not our own. They belong to God, and He desires us to be good stewards of them. We cannot put everything in our bodies and expect them to function well. After some time, the garbage we consume will begin to slow down our bodies. Our bodies are the earth suits given to us so that we may perform God's will in the earth. We must ensure that our natural diet consists of healthy food choices so that we can run our race as God has intended.

THE MIND

"Do not be conformed to this world (this age) [fashioned after and adapted to its external superficial customs] but be ye transformed {changed) by the [entire] renewal of your mind [by its new ideals and its new attitude], so that you may prove [for yourselves] what is good and acceptable and perfect will of God, even the thing which is good and acceptable and perfect [in His sight for you]."

Romans 12:2 (AMP)

The mind is where we think, reason, feel, and remember. It holds the power of imagination, recognition, and appreciation. Our mind is responsible for processing feelings and emotions resulting in attitudes and actions. Studies show that we have anywhere between 50,000 - 70,000 thoughts per day. Our thoughts are guided by what we mentally consume from the world around us. This includes the images we see, the conversations we have, the music we listen to, and even the shows we watch on television. Every day, we make the decision to consume knowledge or junk. Wise men store up knowledge and digest something positive and enriching every day. What we consume and think about determines what comes out of us. Thoughts lead to words, words lead to actions, actions build our character, and our character determines our destiny.

THE SPIRIT

"Hereby we know that we abide in him and he in us, because he hath given us of his Spirit."

1 John 4:13 (ASV)

Last, but certainly not least, is your spirit. *Spirit* is defined as the force within a person that gives the body life, energy, and power. We are spirits that have a mind and live in a body. God gave us His spirit as proof that we live in Him, and He lives in us. Without the spirit, the body is dead. Matthew 4:4 (ASV) says, "Man shall not live by bread alone, but by every word that preceedeth out of the mouth of God." We feed our spirit by reading the word of God. The Bible lets us know that one of the greatest battles we face on a daily is between our flesh and the Spirit. The Spirit is perfect and lacking nothing, however, it must be fed in order to overpower our fleshly desires. God's word gives us the power to deny the temptations of our flesh, and live lives that are pleasing in His sight.

In this book, *Your Destiny Has a Diet,* you will receive nourishment for your mind, spirit, and body. This book doubles as a devotional and a recipe book. After enjoying a message of encouragement and direction, flip to the back of the book and try your hand at one of the recipes. Well, what are you waiting for? Turn to the next page to begin your journey of becoming healthy holistically – mind, body, and spirit.

RECIPES FOR THE SPIRIT & MIND

YOUR DESTINY

"For I know the plans I have for you," says the Lord. "They are plans for good and not for disaster, to give you a future and a hope."

Jeremiah 29:11 (NLT)

You'll Need...
God

His Will & Purpose

Determination

There are many definitions of destiny, the most popular being *the future of a person or a thing determined by previous events.* In Jeremiah 29:11, God lets us know that He indeed has a purpose and a plan for our lives. In fact, we were created for His purpose, usage, and desire. God's purpose for our lives is our true reason for existing. In addition to setting a destiny before us, God also gave us free will. The word of God teaches us that we were created to make choices and we are responsible for the choices we make. We can choose the life He has for us, or we can choose to be disobedient and chase the lives we desire for ourselves. God did not give us free will so that we can live as the world does. Instead, He has given us free will so that we can freely chose to love, obey, and serve Him with our whole lives. Those who accept Christ as Savior have accepted God's plan. His plan is found in His word. To experience the abundant destiny God has planned for us, we must read His Word, follow His instructions, and in all things, pray that the will of the Father will be done. Beloved, you are the only one who can complete your destiny. Decide today to walk boldly along the path God has destined for you.

LET'S PRAY

Lord, we bless Your name. You are the Alpha and Omega. Thank You for Your grace and mercy. We are grateful for the purpose and will You have for our lives. Help us to walk out this plan in obedience. We appreciate You for creating a good plan for us despite our faults. Give us the strength to stay the course.

OBEDIENCE

"But each person is tempted when he is lured and enticed by his own desire. Then desire when it has conceived gives birth to sin, and sin when it is fully grown brings forth death."
James 1:14-15 (ESV)

You'll Need...
God

Faith

Focus

Did you know that teaching a dog to be obedient requires a lot of training? In one dog training method, the dog is at one end of a room while its master stands on the other end. Between the dog and its master is a plate of food. During the training, the master calls for the dog. Studies show that if the dog eyes the food before heeding the call of its master, the training is not yet complete. The dog will go straight for the food instead of running to its master. If the dog keeps its eyes on its master, it won't be tempted to go after the food. In the same light, we as Christians must train ourselves to keep our eyes on our Master and

Heavenly Father, God. The most accurate test of our obedience is our ability to keep our eyes on God in the midst of difficult situations and circumstances. The world will present many great opportunities, however, we will only achieve true success and produce lasting fruit when we follow the instructions of our Master. After Jonah disobeyed God and found himself in the belly of a great fish, the Bible records that Jonah turned his thoughts towards God. After Jonah repented, the fish spit him out on dry land.

Disobedience is expensive. Like Jonah, it will cost us our peace, resources, and success. However, in good times and in bad times, we will find great consolation in focusing on the goodness of God in our present, and His power to help us in our future.

LET'S PRAY

Father, help us to keep our eyes on You in every situation. You are our sanctifier and keeper. Your Word tells us that obedience is better than sacrifice. Help us to obey and trust You in everything we do. Give us the will to step out in faithful obedience when we are called to say or do something out of our comfort zone. Keep our hearts open to Your promptings as we grow in faith and obedience.

CONSISTENCY

"His lord said unto him, Well done, good and faithful [a]servant: thou hast been faithful over a few things, I will set thee over many things; enter thou into the joy of thy lord."
Matthew 25:21 (ASV)

You'll Need...
God

God's Instruction

Determined Heart

Everyone struggles with being consistent from time to time, however, it is the key to living a victorious life. Consistency requires discipline and order. To walk in divine health, our lives must be centered around consistency. We must be consistent in our exercising and eating habits to make it part of our destiny. Being consistent doesn't just happen by chance. It requires us to be intentional about our time, schedule, and energy. When our actions become consistent, so will the results we desire. Matthew 25:21 lets us know that there is a reward for consistency. God will increase and enlarge our territory after we are consistent in our stewardship of what we have been given. If we are not faithful to God over a few things, we cannot expect Him to trust us with bigger things. Many times, we are relentless in our pursuit of something, however, when we receive it, we are not consistent stewards of it. While persistence will allow us to acquire much, only consistency will help us to keep the things we acquire.

LET'S PRAY

Lord, thank You for Your grace and mercy. We give You glory for being consistent and unchanging. Help us to be as consistent as You are. We desire to be consistent in prayer, in reading Your Word, and serving. Help us to focus on You and ignore the distractions that come our way. We know that every good and perfect gift comes from You, so help us to be better stewards of the things You have already given us. We thank You now for making us more consistent.

FOCUS

"Thou wilt keep him in perfect peace, whose mind is stayed on thee."

Isaiah 26:3 (KJV)

You'll Need...
God

His Will & Purpose

1 Determined Heart

In this day and age, there are many things fighting for our attention. We find ourselves distracted by work, keeping up with the trends of the world, social media, celebrities, and more. One of the greatest distractions that cause many to lose their focus on God is money and the lack of it. Sometimes, we find ourselves so consumed with making money to enjoy life and survive that we forget that God is more than able to provide all our needs. In Matthew 6:33, Jesus admonishes us to seek the kingdom of God above everything. In doing so, everything we need will be added unto us. If we are honest, we all struggle with staying focused from time to time. The Bible gives us many examples of people who lost their focus. In Numbers 20, Moses lost focus on God's instruction and struck the rock instead of speaking to it. In Luke 17, nine lepers were so focused on telling others about their healing that they forgot to turn around and thank Jesus for healing them. In Judges 16, Samson got so caught up in a woman that he lost his focus and gave away the secret to his strength. If you've lost your way, decide today to reclaim your focus. Ask God to help you focus on Him and His Purpose for your life.

LET'S PRAY

God, You are great and worthy of all our praise. Today, we thank You for being such a loving and forgiving Father. Even when we lose our way and give our attention to the things of the world, You still open your arms to us when we are ready to return. Thank You, Father. Today, we ask that you would give us clarity about Your Will for our lives. Give us the strength to focus on the path you have set before us.

HUMILITY

"When pride comes, then comes disgrace but with humility comes wisdom."

Proverbs 11:2 (NIV)

You'll Need...
God

His Will &
Purpose

1 Determined
Heart

Humility is an ingredient that is needed in our lives. It is a modest or low view of one's importance. Humility does not mean that we think less of ourselves; it simply means that we think about the needs of others more than our personal desires. Humility is key when it comes to serving God. Every day, we must remember to humble ourselves under the hands of our mighty God. This is the only way we can cheerfully carry out His purpose for our lives. Humility reminds us that there is nothing we can do without our Heavenly Father. It reminds us that our lives are not our own. Pride is the opposite of humility. When we are prideful, we cannot know God or be concerned about His purpose and plan for our lives. Unlike humility, pride tells us that who we are and what we want are more important. This keeps us from learning and accepting the true nature of the Father.

Additionally, humility allows us to remain teachable, regardless of how much we think we know. For example, my mentor/teacher is half my age. If I had been too prideful in my age and wisdom, I would have assumed that my mentor was too young to teach me anything. As a result, I wouldn't be as far along as I am on my journey. However, humility allowed me to see beyond the age gap and realized that God placed my mentor in my life to push me out of my comfort zone. Today, check your heart for pride. If you find that you have been prideful in any situation, ask God to remove it, and give you a spirit of humility in all things.

LET'S PRAY

Lord, thank You for the spirit of humility. Help us not to take pride in our accomplishments, but to remember that all of the honor and glory belongs to You. Help us to recognize when we are stubborn and prideful. Remind us daily that Your Words says that if we are humble, You will lift us up in honor at the right time.

ENDURANCE

"May the God who gives endurance and encouragement give you the same attitude of mind toward each other that Christ Jesus had;"

Romans 15:5 (NIV)

You'll Need...

God

His Will & Purpose

1 Determined Heart

This is not the time to give up. Your situation may be tiring, and you may even feel like there's no hope, but this is not the time to throw in the towel. Life has its share of ups and downs. Sometimes, it seems like as soon as you conquer one trial, life blows another storm your way. Beloved, God never promised that life would be easy. However, He did promise to be with us every step of the way. If you ask, God will give you renewed strength and power. Test and trials only come to make us stronger. God allows difficulty so that we may increase in endurance. In James 1:1, the writer encourages us to count every difficulty as joy.

Looking at the storms of life as joy instead of sadness, allows us to be built by the storm instead of being broken by it. Despite what life may throw in your direction, you must remain hopeful that your breakthrough is on the way. Do not grow weary in well doing and don't you dare give up. In Galatians 6:9, God promises to bless us in the appropriate time, if we stay in the fight!

Anyone can give up, that's easy. However, what determines if you are ready for the blessings headed your way is your ability to endure the storm. God just doesn't want us to *acquire* abundance; He wants us to *keep and maintain it*, and doing so will require us to have endurance.

LET'S PRAY

Lord, we thank You for the storm. We understand that every storm is an opportunity for us to see You move. We believe in our hearts that You will bless the works of our hands if we faint not. Give us the strength to endure the tribulation and press toward the mark. We declare and decree that we shall finish strong!

WISDOM

"The fear of the Lord is the beginning of wisdom and the knowledge of the Holy One is understanding."

Proverbs 9:10 (NIV)

You'll Need...
God

1 Open Heart

2 Listening Ears

We must use wisdom in our daily diets. It is key for making wise decisions in every area of our lives. Wisdom means having experience, knowledge, and good judgment. We often lean on our knowledge and personal experiences to make decisions in life. As a result, we find ourselves deeper in trouble. James 1:5 reminds us that if we desire wisdom, we must seek it from God. We can acquire knowledge from many areas: Sunday School, books, the internet, etc. While knowledge is great, it is just a matter of knowing information. Wisdom is knowing how to apply the information that we know. This wisdom comes from God. When we are faced with difficult decisions, we must condition ourselves to request wisdom from God before we make a move.

LET'S PRAY

Lord, thank You for wisdom and knowledge. We recognize that You are the source of wisdom. Impart divine wisdom within us. Direct our steps and let our ears be inclined to hear Your voice. Correct us when we have gone astray.

PATIENCE

"But those who wait on the Lord shall renew their strength. They shall mount up with wings like eagles, they shall run and not be weary, they shall walk and not faint;"

Isaiah 40:31(NKJV)

You'll Need...
God

Faith

Strength

Waiting for anything can be extremely difficult. Thanks to technology, we barely have to wait for anything. In times past, communication took days, even weeks to be delivered through the mail. Now, we can get a message to those we love in a matter of seconds through email and text message. If we are hungry, we don't have to wait for a good meal to be prepared. We can go to the local fast food joint. The human race has been conditioned to believe that waiting is a thing of the past. As a result, many of us lack patience. In the Bible, we find proof that waiting is not a bad thing and that patience is truly a beautiful trait to possess. From Hannah's patience in waiting for a child to Job's patience in waiting for the storm to end, we see that patience is a necessity when waiting for the things of God. Additionally, patience is more than our ability to wait. It is the attitude we have while we wait. Take a moment and check your attitude with God as you wait. Are your feet tapping anxiously or walking in what God has already revealed to you? Are your hands clenched in frustration or clasped in prayer? Patience is all about our posture in waiting. Remember, if God is causing you to wait, He's either preparing it or preparing you. Regardless, trust that when He delivers what He promised, His timing will be impeccable. In the meantime, keep your hands to the plow and remain hopeful in the promises of the most High!

LET'S PRAY

Father, help us to be patient as we wait for Your promises to manifest on Earth as it is in Heaven. Thank You for granting new strength and patience as we walk with grace at work in our lives. We bless Your name for we know that this season of waiting will only produce more patience, and patience is a reflection of Your love.

A CLEAN HEART

"Search me, O God, and know my heart; Try me and know my anxious thoughts;"

Psalm 139:23(NIV)

You'll Need...
God

Examination

Repentance

In our scripture focus for today, the songwriter makes a great request of God. He asks God to examine His heart. Have you ever gone to the doctor for an exam? Examinations of any kind can be quiet scary. After all, you never know what will be found. Examinations are thorough reviews that go beyond the surface of what one can see on the surface. The songwriter didn't want God to just reveal the surface problems he was struggling with. He wanted God to go beneath the surface and reveal the things that were hiding in the crevices of his heart. Why the trouble? Our hearts are vital to our physical and spiritual wellbeing. Proverbs 4:23 tells us that the issues of life flow from the heart. Lessons from Anatomy and Biology teach us that the heart is responsible for pumping blood throughout the entire body. If our hearts are sick, physically or spiritually, the results would be detrimental to our overall health.

To care for our hearts in the natural, we are told to exercise, eat well, and manage our stress. But, what does God say about caring for our spiritual hearts? Our first step is to make the same request as the songwriter. Ask God to examine your heart and reveal every evil thing that may be lurking in it. After God reveals the areas you need to fix, intentionally seek Him about your healing. Next, you must take the precautions to keep your heart clean from things that don't please God. This is called guarding your heart. We do so by not allowing bitterness, anger, resentment, and lust to set in. We guard our hearts by resisting temptation, remaining humble, loving others, and being quick to forgive. Also, because our minds and hearts are connected and what we think affects our hearts, we must be careful to only think about things that are pure, righteous, and heavenly.

It is impossible for us to carry out the will of the Father without a clean heart. Decide today that you will take the necessary steps to develop and maintain a clean and healthy heart.

LET'S PRAY

Gracious God, thank You for creating in us a clean heart and renewing a right spirit within us. Thank You for washing, purging, and removing all doubts inside our hearts and minds. We give You glory for making a clean heart available to us, and with Your help, we will maintain its cleanliness every day.

REST

"It is in vain that you rise up early and go late to rest, eating the bread of anxious toil; for he gives to his beloved sleep."
Psalm 127:2 (ESV)

You'll Need...
God

Faith

We all need rest. Even God rested. The Bible tells us in the book of Genesis that after six days of creating the world, God rested on the seventh day. In the same manner, we must develop a balance between work and rest. Rest doesn't just come at the end of our life's journey. We should also rest while we are on the battlefield for the Lord. Exodus 34:21 (NLT) says, "Six days are set aside for work, but on the Sabbath day you must rest, even during the season of planting and harvest." This means that even in the midst of your working, you must allow yourself moments to rest and recharge. We don't always need coffee or an energy drink to keep us sharp. The truth is, sometimes we just need to allow our minds and bodies to rest. Rest is a key part in your diet for your destiny. Without adequate rest, the body cannot function at its best. Beloved, remember that you are not a machine. You are a human being and to perform at your best *you need to rest!*

LET'S PRAY

God, we desperately need You to help us balance between working and resting. We understand that in order to effectively carry out Your will in the earthly realm, we must allow our bodies to rest. Thank You for showing us in Your word that You took a rest. We come against the spirit of guilt and anxiety that attacks us when we rest. We decree and declare that we shall peacefully rest and rejuvenate in Your presence without fear of failure.

.

YOUR PURPOSE

"For by him were all things created, that are in heaven, and that are in earth, visible and invisible, whether they be thrones, or dominions, or principalities, or powers: all things were created by him, and for him:"

Colossians 1:16 (NLT)

You'll Need...
God

His Will

The Desire To Please God

Purpose is the reason why we have breath in our bodies. Contrary to popular belief, our purpose isn't about the possessions we obtain, the success we achieve, or experiencing happiness. Those things are great, and there's nothing wrong with desiring those accomplishments. However, those acquirements come secondary to the purpose of God for your life. So many people live their entire lives chasing things that have no value. In fact, graves all across the world are filled with the bodies of people who accomplished everything except their God-given purpose. I don't know about you, but to think of leaving this earth without doing what I was created to do in it is absolutely scary.

Spend some time with God about your purpose. If you feel that you are already operating in your God-given purpose, ask God to realign your focus where needed. If not, ask God to lead you to His purpose for your life. Again, purpose is the reason why we were created in the first place. If you are not operating in your purpose, you aren't living, you are simply existing. Get in touch with God's purpose for your life while you still can!

LET'S PRAY

God, we understand that we are the works of Your hands. We were created to fulfill Your desires in the earth. Our lives are not our own. We belong to You. Use us as You see fit. Quiet the desires of our flesh so that we may clearly hear Your Will for our lives.

TRUST

"Casting all your cares upon him; for the caret for you."
I Peter 5:7 (NLT)

You'll Need...
God

Faith

Prayer

In Philippians 4:6, the Apostle Paul admonishes us to worry about nothing, but instead, bring our desires to God in prayer with gratitude. Why does Paul tell us to do such a thing? Surely he didn't know about all the worries we face on a daily basis. We have bills to pay, loved ones to care for, deadlines at work, and responsibilities to fulfill at church. It seems nearly impossible not to worry about something.

First, understand that there is a difference between worrying and being concerned about something. When we are concerned, we are aware that there is something we must take care of. The Bible tells us that God himself is concerned about us. However, worry is the act of being uneasy and anxious about the future. Worry and anxiety lead to stressful days, sleepless night, and health issues. God does not desire us to worry. Worry alludes to a lack of faith in God as it causes us to begin to look for answers in things and people.

As Christians, we have nothing to worry about. Our future is secure, the victory has been won, and we have an end to expect. The Bible tells us that God has purposed a prosperous future for us. There are so many scriptures that encourage us not to worry. Each one cancels out any anxiety that we may ever have. Don't believe me? Let's check out a few.

Are you faced with a bad result you cannot get around? Don't worry, God's word Says:

> *"And we know that all things work together for good to them that love God, to them who are the called according to his purpose."*
>
> *Romans 8:28 (KJV)*

Are you worried about a bill or a need not being met? Don't worry, God's word says,

> *"And my God will meet all your needs according to the riches of his glory in Christ."*
>
> *Philippians 4:19 (NIV)*

Are you worried about something bad happening to you or someone you love? Don't worry. God's word says,

> *"No weapon that is formed against thee shall prosper; and every tongue that shall rise against thee in judgment thou shalt condemn. This is the heritage of the servants of the LORD, and their righteousness is of me, saith the LORD."*
>
> Isaiah 54:17 (KJV)

As you can see, there is a scripture for every worry we could ever have. Instead of worrying, go to the word of God and find scriptures for your situation. God knew that we would be faced with trials and tribulations of all kinds. For that reason, He inspired men to record His word so that we would always have it to refer to. Additionally, He sent His Holy Spirit to comfort us. Do you see how intentional and concerned our God is? Before you ever had a problem, He already had a solution. You just have to trust and have faith in His Word. Ask yourself this: When was the last time God failed you? Never! God has everything under control. Trust His plan. Don't worry. Just pray.

LET'S PRAY

God, You make all things well. We don't have to worry about anything. Thank You for giving us peace that surpasses all understanding. We know that you are perfecting everything that concerns us because you love, and care for us. Thank You for being our protector, shield and provider.

PREPARATION

"But in your hearts honor Christ the Lord as holy, always being prepared to make a defense to anyone who asks you for a reason for the hope that is in you; yet do it with gentleness and respect;"

1 Peter 3:15 (ESV)

You'll Need...
God

His Will & Purpose

Trust

As Christians, we sometimes make the mistake of believing that God-given assignments are without toil. When God places goals and desires within us, and we trust Him enough to walk toward them, it can be discouraging to encounter obstacles. Beloved, those obstacles don't mean that you are going in the wrong direction. Sometimes, the path to fulfilling God's will is filled with roadblocks, thorns, and difficulty. God allows these obstacles, not to deter us, but to prepare us for what is ahead. Instead of viewing obstacles as stop signs, we must learn to view them as opportunities to learn and train for what is ahead. We may not always understand God's method of preparation, but we must always trust that He knows best. Nothing worth having ever comes easy or without opposition. Storms will come, and our fears will be confronted. However, there is hope. God has given us the power to overcome every obstacle before us. After all, the victory has already been won! Trust that God has equipped you and will continue to equip you along the way.

LET'S PRAY

God, thank You for preparing us for everything You desire us to acquire and accomplish for Your Kingdom. May we be steadfast in our pursuit of Your purpose for our lives. Transform our thinking and mentality. Endow us with the strength to press through difficult moments. We know that You will never fail or abandon us. With You, all things are possible.

RELATIONSHIP

"Jesus told him, "I am the way, the truth, and the life. No one can come to the Father except through me."

John 14:6 (NLT)

You'll Need...
God

Intentionality

1 Open Heart

A relationship with God is the only thing that will quench our soul's longing. In John 6:35, Jesus says to us, "I am the bread of life. He who comes to me will never go hungry and he who believes in me will never be thirsty." Until we learn God, we will remain unsatisfied with life. No amount of money, success, or achievement will make us content. Our deepest desire is to know God and have a relationship with Him because were created to worship and please Him. It's in our DNA. Before the death of Jesus Christ, we had to go through priests to communicate with God. Our sinful lives would not permit us to be in His presence. Jesus came so that each of us would know and understand God in a personal way. We don't need another human being to atone for our sins, or seek the Father on our behalf. We can go boldly before the throne of God. We can get to know Him and experience His presence on our own.

Decide to develop the relationship that will quench your hunger and thirst. Understand that a true relationship with the Father will bring clarity, unexplainable peace, true joy, and purpose into your life. This relationship will change your life and your view of life.

LET'S PRAY

What a mighty God we serve! We acknowledge your sovereignty and seek you today for a deeper relationship with you. Help us to walk in Your righteousness every day. Give us a desire for Your Will and Your Way.

STILLNESS

"Be still, and know that I am God: I will be exalted among the heathen, I will be exalted in the earth."

Psalm 46:10 (KJV)

You'll Need...
God

2 Closed Lips

2 Listening Ears

In the Greek, the word *still* is *Ακόμη*. Its translation means to be silent, or as we would say, Shut Up! I know "Shut Up" can be a harsh statement for many, but the truth is, sometimes that's exactly what we need to do. Moments of quietness and stillness is key to hearing God's instruction clearly. We can become so busy saying and doing nothing that we miss what God is requesting of us. God tells us to be still so that we can hear from Him and receive love, peace, and guidance. Meditating on God's Word is a great way to quiet the world around you and hear from God. Take a moment today and spend some quiet time with God. Silence your worries, fears, anxieties, and to-do lists. Allow your quiet time with God to rejuvenate you and clear your vision of your future!

LET'S PRAY

Father, in the name of Jesus, lead us to the place in our souls where there is peace, calmness, and tranquility. Then Lord, allow Your gentle spirit of kindness infiltrate this land. Teach us to follow Your voice in all we do.

.

PROCESS

"Be patient therefore, brothers, until the coming of the lord. Behold, the farmer waits for his precious fruit of the earth, being patient over it, until it receives the early and late rain."

James 5:7 (NLT)

You'll Need...
God

Patience

Endurance

A process is a series of actions or steps taken to achieve a certain end. Reaping a harvest of any kind is a process. We all want to see a harvest, but we don't always like to endure the process it requires. Beloved, understand that there is no such thing as an overnight harvest. First we are to till the ground, then we plant the seeds, and finally believe God for our harvest. If we sow seeds of health, healing, and balance, in time we will reap a harvest of weight loss and healthy living. If we sow seeds of time, investment, and integrity, we will soon reap the harvest of prosperity. Every harvest you desire has a seed requirement.

Though it may seem like your seeds are taking their precious time to sprout – keep sowing. Just as any seed has to go through maturation, our seeds of destiny must go through the same process before they become ripe and fully developed. Celebrate the progress you've made. Remember that each step forward is a step forward, no matter how far it takes you. Know that there will never be a more perfect time to sow seeds than right now.

LET'S PRAY

God, we thank You for patience and endurance to continue planting. We thank You in advance for the plentiful harvest headed in our direction. We know that this harvest will not only supply our needs, but it will also enable us to bless others. In faith, we hold steadfast to Your Word and believe that we will reap if we faint not!

HEALING

"Jesus answered, "Everyone who drinks this water will be thirsty again, but whoever drinks the water I give them will never thirst. Indeed, the water I give them will become in them a spring of water welling up to eternal life."

John 4:13-14 (NIV)

You'll Need...
God

Honesty

Patience

Intentionality

In John 4, Jesus encounters a woman desiring to fulfill her physical and spiritual thirst. Before her encounter with Jesus, she had attempted several times to quench her thirst. Unfortunately, no man could fix the void in her heart...*not even the one she was currently with.* At the well, Jesus recognized her brokenness and offered her a drink from the well of living water. Like the woman at the well, we have tried to fill the voids and broken places in our hearts with people, jobs, and expensive assets. While these things bring us temporary fulfillment, we are eventually left wanting and desiring more. The word *temporary* is defined as something that only lasts for a limited period of time. Many of us have attempted to put Band-Aids on places that need true healing, not temporary fixes.

That healing can only come through Jesus Christ. We must be willing to forsake the temporary fixes we've used in the past and depend solely upon Him for healing and transformation.

It is God's plan and desire that we are healed. Healing is a vital part of our diet and is key to our physical and spiritual well-being. Welcome God to heal and fill every void in your heart. Just as Jesus offered living water to the woman at the well, He is offering living water to you today. Will you drink from the well that never runs dry?

LET'S PRAY

Father, we bless Your name for Your healing power! Deliver us from all afflictions. Fill every void in our hearts. Allow us to see the power of Your healing. We are grateful that Your Word is true, You will never leave us or forsake us. We shall drink of You, Lord, and never thirst again. In You, there is the fullness of joy. Thank You for restoration! We love You, Lord.

GOOD WORKS

"In the same way, let your light shine before others, so that they may see your good works and give glory to your Father who is in heaven."

Matthew 5:16 (ESV)

You'll Need...
God

An Understanding of Who You Are

Endurance

As we discussed before, we were created to fulfill the desires of God on Earth. As God's workmanship we must study and practice God's ways in order to fulfill our responsibilities. On our jobs, we seek our bosses for instruction, guidance, and training. This is the only way we can successfully complete the job we were employed to do. In the same way, we must seek God about the works He created us to do. To keep ourselves fit for the work of the Kingdom, we must pray, meditate, fast, and read God's word daily. Unlike the things we do for the world, the work we complete for God has everlasting benefits. Though it is not always easy, it is always worth it. God designed us to do good works. Let's show the Father how grateful we are by putting our hands to the plow and completing the tasks in which He created us to do!

LET'S PRAY

Lord, thank You for creating us in Your Image. We give You glory for designing us to be creative and skillful for Your glory. The word declares that eyes have not seen, ears have not heard, and no mind has imagined the things that You have prepared us for because we love You. We believe that it is so! Give us the focus to not turn to the left or right, but to push ahead into all that You've prepared for us.

MORE TRUST

He has made everything beautiful in its time

Ecclesiastes 3:11 (NLT)

You'll Need...
God

His Timing

Endurance

Are you going through a difficult time right now, and you want it to be over? Have you been waiting for a breakthrough and you have grown frustrated in your waiting? Beloved, you are not alone. There will be many times in our lives when we wish things would move at a faster pace. Nevertheless, we must trust God's timing. He goes before us and makes the crooked roads straight and all rough paths smooth. If you are still waiting for the manifestation of God's promises, there is a lesson you still need to learn. God is purposeful in His timing. His Word tells us that He will not withhold anything good from us. If it has not come, it is possible that it is not good for you right now.

Instead of putting your attention on God's Hands, take a look at your own hands. God is perfect, He cannot lie, and He always does exactly what He promises. However, this is not always true for us. What are your hands working on? Have you done what God has instructed? What was the last thing God told you to do? Your waiting is only in vain if you are not positioning yourself to receive what you are waiting for. Do a quick assessment of your posture. Is there something you can do as you wait?

LET'S PRAY

Father, thank You for Your perfect timing. Your word says that one day with You is like one thousand years, and a thousand years is like one day. God, with our finite minds we can't begin to comprehend a thousand years, but we trust Your sovereignty and Your timing in every area of our lives. Teach us to be patient. Bring to our remembrance any assignment we have not completed. Give us focus and clarity in this waiting season.

PEACE

"Peace I leave with you; my peace I give you. I do not give to you as the world gives. Do not let your hearts be troubled and do not be afraid."

John 14:27 (NIV)

You'll Need...
God

His Will &
Purpose

1 Determined
Heart

Peace is a fruit of the spirit. As believers, we are obligated to let the peace of God rule in our hearts. Jesus is our Prince of peace, therefore, we can have the peace of God no matter what circumstances we are going through. God is Alpha and Omega, and He knows our beginning to our end. Nothing happens to us that He does not see or allow. Though the enemy attacks to kill us, only the purposes of God will prevail. When we realize these truths, we are able to look turmoil in the face and still have peace. In Philippians 4:7, the Apostle Paul admonishes us not to worry, but instead, submit our requests to God.

In doing so, God will grant us a peace that surpasses all understanding. Paul doesn't say that God will answer our petitions immediately. Sometimes, God will give us peace before He gives us the promise. In these moments, we must remind ourselves that we serve a God who loves us and is concerned about us. We have no reason to fear or worry about the outcome of our lives.

The storms of life will blow. As long as we have breath in our bodies, we will face trials and tribulation. In the midst of it all, we need not fret or worry. God will indeed fight all of our battles. As He wars on your behalf, allow His peace to guard your heart and your mind.

LET'S PRAY

God, we thank You for peace that surpasses all understanding. Thank You for granting us peace in every situation in our lives. In the midst of storms, help us to stay focused on You. Though debris is flying all around us, we chose to keep our eyes glued to Your Promises.

SACRIFICE

"Honor the Lord with your wealth, with the first fruits of all of your crops."

Proverbs 3:9 (NLT)

You'll Need...
God

1 Willing Heart

Selflessness

Many Christians fail to realize that sowing and reaping is a major principle of the kingdom. God does not desire us to give because He lacks. Instead, giving sharpens our ability to trust and obey God. When it comes to the subject of giving and making sacrifices, we typically think of money. While giving God a percentage of our monetary earnings is necessary, this is not the only way we give. God also desires us to give our time, talent, and effort. God's word says that what we make happen for others, He will make happen for us. He has not placed us on the earth to be selfish and tight-fisted. He desires us to help others when we can. While we might not always reap *where* we sowed, we will always reap *what* we sowed. If you are in need of assistance, help others. If you desire support, support the efforts of others. If you want increase, sow increase into others. While those people may not sow back into you, you will reap exactly what you need according to what you have sown. Again, sowing and reaping is a principle. It either works for us, or against us depending on our obedience.

Giving is not only beneficial, but it is also one way we worship God. When we give, we remind God that we know where our true help comes from. Giving reminds us that God is able to supply our needs beyond what's in our bank accounts. Giving allows us to truly witness the abundance, favor, and grace of God.

LET'S PRAY

Father, thank You for being the perfect role model for giving. You have given us so much, and we are grateful. We thank You now for the greatest gift, Your Son, Jesus Christ. Now God, teach us to give as freely as You do. Show us how we can sow our resources, time, and effort into others. Incline our hearts to give cheerfully into Your Kingdom.

ENCOURAGEMENT

"And David was greatly distressed; for the people spake of stoning him, because the soul of all the people was grieved, every man for his sons and for his daughters: but David encouraged himself in the Lord his God."

1 Samuel 30:6 (KJV)

You'll Need...
God

His Word

1 Open Heart

We all need encouragement on this journey called life. Sometimes, we won't get the encouragement we need from those around us. We will have to look within and encourage ourselves in the Lord. How do we encourage ourselves in the Lord? We start by taking a look at our lives and acknowledging how far God has already brought us. One of the enemy's favorite tactics is to magnify our situations, problems, and current storms. He desires to make us feel defeated. However, taking a look at God's resume in our lives will remind us that our God is mighty and victorious. He cannot and will not fail.

Next, we must immerse ourselves in the Word of God. The Bible is filled with encouragement. When negative thoughts pop into our minds, we must make them submit to the word of God. This is difficult if you are unaware of what God's word says. Memorize scriptures that reveal the promises of God. When you are feeling low or discouraged, recite those scriptures aloud until you begin to feel better.

In addition to reviewing God's resume and reciting His promises, you must also ask God to change your perspective of the situation you are going through. There is a purpose in everything God allows you to encounter. Remember His word promises to make every situation work for our good. Instead of saying that things are happening to you, believe that everything is happening for you!

When there is no one around to wipe your tears and push you through, take that opportunity to encourage yourself in the Lord.

LET'S PRAY

Father, thank You for encouraging us through Your Word. Even with people all around us, we can sometimes still feel alone. In those moments, remind us to go within and seek You. We come against the spirit of defeat, and believe in our hearts that we are always victorious in You! Thank You for the storms that teach us how to war in the spirit. Though they were uncomfortable, we are stronger because of them. Finally, Father, thank You for removing the blinders and allowing us to see the truth in every situation we encounter.

VICTORY

"When we go through deep waters and great trouble, I will be with you. When you go through rivers of difficulty, you will not drown! When you walk through the fire of oppression, you will not be burned up; the flames will not consume you."

Isaiah 43:2 (NLT)

You'll Need...
God

Faith

Perseverance

What would you do if you knew you could not lose? If you are in Christ, the victory has already been won on your behalf. Though the storms may come, you still have an expected end. When life flips everything around you upside down, fret not. God has already purposed a prosperous future before you. You can make it, and you will make it if you trust and believe in God. You are not a victim, you are victorious! Claim your victory today by pressing through the storms and leaning into God. Beloved, you can't lose with God. Hold your head high and speak as a victor. Let the words from your mouth prophesy what you don't see. Decree and declare the victory, for it already belongs to you. Regardless of what you see, the battle has already been won. You are victorious.

LET'S PRAY

God, we trust that You know everything we are currently dealing with. We refuse to believe the bad reports of the enemy, the doctors, the bank, the college, or those around us. We chose to believe Your report. It is well! Thank You for going before us, fighting the battle, and claiming the victory on our behalf

FREEDOM

"Now the Lord is that Spirit: and where the Spirit of the Lord is, there is liberty."

2nd Corinthians 3:17 (KJV)

You'll Need...
God

Freedom is defined as the state of not being imprisoned or enslaved. In Jesus Christ, we are free from every mental, physical, and spiritual bondage. Unfortunately, many of us are enslaved by the mistakes we've made in the past. Beloved, you must choose today that you will accept the freedom that is in Christ Jesus. We've all made some mistakes. Even if we don't care to admit it, we've all done and said things that we are not proud of. Nevertheless, the Bible tells us that if any man be in Christ Jesus, He is a new creature and the things of his past are passed away. All things are new in Christ. This means that you are no longer bound to the mistakes you made. In His word, God tells us that when we repent of our sins, He forgives us. He casts them into a sea of forgetfulness. He removes them from us as far as the east is from the west. While others may not so easily forget our transgressions, and may hold our past against us, it is not our job to prove them wrong. We should focus on proving God right! So shake off the chains of the past, and move forward into your future in the righteousness of God!

LET'S PRAY

God, we thank You that we have victory over every stronghold. Help us turn from our wicked ways and live life freely in You. Give us the strength to look beyond the whispers of others. Incline our ears to only hear the truth You speak about us. Release us now from the mistakes of our past. Show us how to live in You as new creatures.

DIRECTION

"The steps of a good man is ordered by God."

Psalms 37:23 (KJV)

You'll Need...
God

His Word

1 Obedient Heart

When I was a child, one of my favorite hymns to sing was, *Where He Leads Me.* The songwriter wrote, "Where He leads me, I will follow, I'll go with Him all the way." Though I sang this song often in my youth, I really didn't understand the meaning of it until now. Life will present many options, trials, opportunities, ups, and downs. However, despite the twists and turns, if we follow His direction, we will accomplish the plan He has for us. It is impossible to go wrong when we are following God. Being confronted with obstacles does not mean we have veered off from God's path. Obstacles are necessary for our preparation and development. However, if we find ourselves in sin, we can be sure we have diverted from God's path for our lives. His word tells us that He leads us into righteousness – not temptation.

When the world gives you many routes you can take on your journey, chose to follow the path of God. Though His path may not be the easiest, it is the only one that will lead to everlasting life.

LET'S PRAY

God, thank You for leading us down paths of righteousness. Help us as we determine in our hearts to follow You wherever You take us. God, we desire to plant our feet in our faith in You. We decree and declare that we will not veer off the path You have set before us no matter how tempting the paths of the world may appear.

COMMUNICATION

"But when you pray, go into your room and shut the door and pray to your Father who is in secret. And your Father who sees in secret will reward you."

Matthew 6:6 (ESV)

You'll Need...
God

Prayer

His Word

Prayer is how we communicate with God. We don't just pray when trouble comes our way. Prayer should be done daily. In natural relationships, communication is key. It is even more important in our relationship with God. When we communicate with one another, one person doesn't do all of the talking. Prayer is the same way. It is a dialogue – not a monologue. Many Christians forsake the beautiful benefits of communing with the Father simply because they forget to be quiet and listen for God's response. God listens to our prayers, answers our prayers, and moves in response to our prayers. When done correctly, prayer can change the trajectory of our lives and help us to develop a deeper relationship with God. If you are not sure how to pray, begin with studying the Model Prayer. It can be found in Matthew 6:5-15. Additionally, many other accounts of prayer can be found in Kings 4 3:36, Mark 9:29, Psalms 6:9-10, James 1:5, and Daniel 4:35.

When you pray, remember to pray the will of God which is found in the word of God. Praying the word of God brings God in remembrance of His word. This makes our prayers even more powerful. It is impossible to have peace without prayer. If you desire more peace and closer communication with God, start by increasing your communication with the Father. Instead of calling a friend to talk about your day, talk to God. He wants to hear from you. If your prayer life is not as strong as you would like it to be, challenge yourself to pray to God at least three times a day until it becomes normal to you. You don't have to be in a prayer closet, at church, or on your knees to pray. While there is nothing wrong with it, God is more concerned about your heart posture than your physical posture when you pray. You can pray in your car, on the treadmill, while you cook, and even as you are taking a quiet walk. Prayer is the place to believe God and receive from God. Commit to increasing your communication with the Father today.

LET'S PRAY

Loving Father, how wonderful it is to commune with You throughout our day. We thank You now for the ability to pray and communicate with You. We are not perfect, we don't know all the scriptures to say, and we sometimes don't know the words to say to You, but we seek You earnestly now with our whole hearts. Teach us how to communicate with You better. We desire to draw closer to You. God, may the words of our mouths and the meditation of our hearts be acceptable in Your sight.

RESTORATION

"I will restore to you the years that the swarming locusts has eaten, the hopper, the destroyer, and the cutter, my great army, which I sent among you "you shall eat in plenty and be satisfied and praise the name of the lord your god who has dealt wondrously with you. And my people shall never again be put to shame."

Joel 2:25-26 (ESV)

You'll Need...

God

1 Open Heart

Faith

There are many stories in the Bible of God's restoration power. Perhaps one of the greatest stories being that of our friend, Job. The Bible says that Job was an upright man. Despite his decision to live righteously, Job endured a great deal of turmoil and strife. While we've all seen our share of trouble, I daresay we haven't experienced nearly as much as Job. Job loved God, however, after losing his children, family, friends, possessions, reputation, and health, he had some questions. He couldn't understand why God allowed him to experience such heartache. Job questioned God, but he never cursed Him. He held on to his faith in God. As a reward, God restored Job and gave him double for his trouble. Now, let's talk about you. Are you going through a tough season? Is your health under attack? Is your money a little funny? Does it seem like all your friends have walked away? Have you lost your job and can't seem to find employment? Is your family going crazy? Are you experiencing a little of all the above? If you answered yes to any of these questions, you are in the perfect position to witness and experience the restoration power of God.

God can and will restore you if you will stick to your guns and keep the faith. Despite what the doctors may say, you are not beyond complete healing. You have not lost so much that you cannot start over. You are not too old to try. Your reputation is not beyond repair. We serve a God who holds time in His hands. The heart of the king is in His hands, and He can turn it how He pleases. All the riches of the world belong to Him. He is the creator, and the Great I Am. Nothing is out of His reach or out of His control. There isn't anything our God is incapable of doing!

So my friend, be encouraged. Hold fast to His promises and His word. Keep praying, fasting, and seeking. Cry out if you must, but don't give up. God shall restore!

LET'S PRAY

God, thank You for being a Restorer. Thank You for restoring our health, wellness, strength, peace, and the years that the locusts had eaten up. Thank You for making all things new and complete. Thank You for sustaining us even when we wander away from You. Thank You for steadfast love and tender mercies that are new every morning. No one repairs like You do. God, we lay our doubts and worries at Your feet. We bind every lie from hell and loose the peace of Your truth over our minds. We thank You in advance for how You will turn our lives around for Your glory. God, You are great! You deserve all of the praise. We magnify You and anticipate seeing Your mighty unchanging hand!

DESTROY PROCRASTINATION

"Work hard and cheerfully at whatever you do, as though you were working for the Lard rather than people."

Colossians 3:23 (NLT)

You'll Need...
God

Determination

Focus

As I prepared to write this last devotional, God instructed me to write about an area in which I still struggle. I couldn't help but chuckle. I knew exactly what He was talking about. Procrastination kept me from completing this book for so many years. Even after I began writing, it took me nearly nine months to complete what God had already spoken to me about. Procrastination is the act of delaying or postponing something. Procrastination is when we put off the tasks of today until we feel like completing them tomorrow. We all deal with procrastination from time to time. It affects those in the body of Christ who are creative, or have been given great vision from God.

While it may appear as laziness, procrastination can also be rooted in fear or anxiety. Sometimes, we are so afraid of what's next, that we procrastinate doing what God is saying now.

If you battle with procrastination, know that you can be free from it. Jesus died for your procrastination as well! To break the chain of procrastination you must become intentional about completing things in the timing in which God has told you to do so. His word says that obedience is better than sacrifice. When we procrastinate, we disobey God's instruction. Even though we may eventually get it done, delayed obedience is still disobedience. The timing of God is sensitive, and we must be sure to act on the things He instructs us to act upon. Missing the timing of God can be detrimental to our next season. Decide today to get free from the struggle of procrastination. There is so much more in store for you.

LET'S PRAY

God, every day is a blessing. While nothing we can't pay You for every day You bless us with, the least we can do is make the most of every day, minute, second, and hour You grant us. We decide today to be about Our Father's business, and use every day to fulfill the tasks You have set before us. As we draw closer to You, make us more consistent. We come against the spirit of fear, procrastination, and laziness. We decree and declare that they shall no longer hold up our productivity. We will operate in excellence and integrity, In Jesus' Name!

RECIPES FOR THE BODY

Vegetable & Beef Soup

You'll Need...

3 or 4 med white potatoes diced in squares
1 can of kennel corn (drained)
1 can of lima beans (drained)
3 cans of diced tomatoes
1 onion chopped
1 small can of tomato sauce
1 can of carrots (drained)
2 med bags of Sweet Pict gumbo mix
2 lbs. of ground beef or turkey (Browned and seasoned drained excess grease
½ stick of real butter (optional)

Directions

Bring the potatoes to a boil with 2 cups of water.

Mix all ingredients in a large pot.

Cook soup for 30 to 40 minutes at medium heat.

Let soup cool and serve.

Chicken Noodle Soup

You'll Need...

2 tbsp. of butter
½ c chopped onions
½ c chopped celery
(3) 14 oz. cans of chicken broth
1 can of vegetable broth
½ lb. of cooked chicken breast
1 ½ c of egg noodles
1 sliced carrot
½ tsp. dried basil
½ tsp. dried oregano
Salt & pepper to taste

Directions

Add all ingredients in a large pot over medium heat.

Melt butter. Cook onion and celery in butter until just tender, maybe 3 mins.

Pour in chicken and vegetable broth and stir in chicken, noodles, carrots, basil, oregano, salt and pepper.

Bring to a boil then reduce heat and simmer 15 mins before serving.

Shirley McConico

Cabbage Soup

You'll Need...

(2) 16 oz. cans whole peeled tomatoes with liquid
1 large head of cabbage chopped
1 pack dry onion mix (envelope)
(11) 5oz can green beans, drained
2 quarts of tomato juice
2 green bell peppers diced
10 stalks celery chopped
(11) 4oz can of beef broth

Directions

Place carrots, onions, tomatoes, cabbage, green beans, peppers, and celery in a large pot.

Add onion soup mix, tomato juice, beef broth, and enough water to cover vegetables.

Simmer until vegetables are tender.

This can be kept in the refrigerator for 8-10 days.

Potato Soup

You'll Need...

6 med potatoes peeled and diced
6 celery stalks diced
2 quarts of water
2 carrots shredded
1 med onion chopped
6 tbsps. butter
6 tbsps. all-purpose flour
1 tsp salt
½ tsp pepper
1½ c whole milk
2 chicken bouillon cubes

Directions

In a large pot cook potatoes, carrots and celery in water with bouillon cubes until tender.

Sauté onions in butter until soft.

Stir in flour, salt and pepper.

Gradually adding milk, stirring constantly until desired consistency.

Makes 8-10 servings.

Red Bean Soup

You'll Need...

1 lb. of smoke sausage, sliced
1 ½ quarts of water
2 (15 ounce) cans red kidney beans drained
1 (15 ounce) can tomato sauce
1 med onion, chopped
1 large potatoes, peeled and diced
2 carrots, sliced
1 stalk celery, chopped
2 cloves garlic, minced
1/8 tsp salt & pepper
1/8 tsp. paprika
½ c uncooked macaroni
½ sm. head cabbage, thickly sliced
2 tbsp. lemon juice

Directions

Cook sausage in a large Dutch oven until browned.

Drain and return to the oven, and add water and next 10 ingredients.

Bring to a boil; reduce heat, and simmer, uncovered for 1 ½ hours.

Stir in macaroni, cabbage, and lemon juice then continue to cook for 30 min.

Makes 3 ½ quarts.

Brunswick Stew

You'll Need...

1 pork roast
1 chicken
1 can cream corn
1 cans whole kernel corn
6 potatoes
2 onions
1 large can tomatoes or 2 small cans
Salt and pepper to taste

Directions

Cook roast & chicken until real tender.

Chop into small pieces.

Chop onions and potatoes.

Add all other ingredients.

Add pork broth as needed.

Cook on low heat.

Cheese & Broccoli Soup

You'll Need...
4 cups broccoli (florets)
4 cloves of garlic (minced)
3 cups of chicken broth
1 cup of heavy cream
3 ½ cups cheese (shredded bag)

Directions

In a large pot over medium heat sauté garlic for one minute.

Add chicken broth, heavy cream and chopped broccoli.

Increase heat and simmer for 15 20 minutes, until broccoli is tender.

Add cheese gradually, stirring until all cheese is used up.

Remove from heat once cheese is melted.

Mom's Beef Stew

You'll Need...

1 lb. beef stew cut into 1 inch cubes
1 med onion
3 carrots
3 to 4 medium potatoes
1 c water
1 large can of tomato sauce
1/3 call-purpose flour
1 tbsp. salt
1 tsp. sugar
1 tsp oregano
2bay leaves

Directions

Heat oven to 325°Mix all ingredients in 4 quart Dutch oven.

Cover and bake 2 hours, stirring once.

Let bake for 1 hour longer or until beef and vegetables are tender.

Pea Soup

You'll Need...

2 ¼ c dried split peas
2 quarts water
1 ½lb.ham bone or shanks
2 small onions sliced thinly
½ tsp salt
¼ tsp black pepper
3 celery stalks (chopped)
3 carrots chopped
1 potato diced

Directions

Add all ingredients in a large stock pot cover peas with 2 quarts water and soak overnight.

Once peas are soaked add ham bone, onion salt and pepper.

Cover bring to boil then simmer for 1 ½ hours stirring occasionally.

Remove bone; cut off meat and return to soup.

Add celery carrots and potatoes.

Cook slowly, uncovered for 30 to 40 minutes or until vegetables are tender.

Asparagus Soup

You'll Need...

1lbs. green asparagus
1lg onion chopped
1tbsp. butter (unsalted)
5 c of chicken broth
½ c heavy cream
¾ tsp fresh lemon juice

Directions

Cut tips from top of asparagus cut remains into ¼ in pieces.

Cook onion in 2tbsp butter in a four quart heavy pot over moderately low heat, stirring, until softened.

Add asparagus pieces and salt and pepper to taste.

Then cook, stirring, 5 minutes.

Add 5 cups broth and simmer, covered, until asparagus Is tender, 15-20 minutes.

While soup simmers, cook reserved asparagus tips in, boiling salted water until tender 3 to 4 minutes, then drain.

Puree soup in batches In a blender until smooth, transferring to a boil (be cautious when blending hot liquids), return to pan.

Stir in cream then add broth to thin soup to desired consistency.

Season with salt and pepper.

Bring soup to a boil and whisk remaining tbsp. of butter. Add lemon juice and garnish with asparagus tops.

Shirley McConico

Tuna Casserole

You'll Need...

2cans of tuna
1large onion (chopped}
1 bell pepper (chopped)
2cups of macaroni (boiled & drained)
4 oz. pimentos
1 can of cream of chicken
1 can of cream of mushroom
16 oz. sour cream
1 ½ c Ritz crackers for topping (crushed)
1 c cheese (shredded)

Directions

Stir ingredients together.

Bake at 325 until done.

Sausage & Hash Brown Casserole

You'll Need...

2 lbs. pork or turkey sausage
1 cup sour cream
8 oz. French onion dip
1 can cream of chicken soup
2 cups shredded cheese
1 bag 30 oz. hash browns (thawed)
1 cup chopped onion
½ c chopped bell pepper (optional)
Salt & pepper to taste

Directions

Brown sausage.

Mix all ingredients together.

Put half of the cheese mixture at the bottom of a 9x13 Pyrex dish.

Top with half of the sausage.

Then top with remaining cheese mixture and remaining sausage.

Bake at 350°for 1 hour or until done.

Chicken Casserole

You'll Need...

4 large chicken breasts, cooked & chopped
2 cans vegetable-all, drained
2 cans cream of chicken soup
1 medium onion, chopped finely
1 can sliced water chestnuts drained
(1) 8oz carton sour cream
1 cup grated cheese
Ritz crackers
Butter

Directions

Place ingredients in large baking dish.

Cover with crushed crackers and dot with butter.

Bake at 400° until mixture begins to bubble and turns brown.

Hamburger Casserole

You'll Need...

1 ½ lb. of lean ground beef
3 med. Potatoes sliced thin
1 can of cream of mushroom soup
½ c chopped onions
¾ cup milk
Salt and Pepper to taste
1 cup shredded cheddar cheese

Directions

Preheat oven to 350 degrees.

Brown the ground beef and drain fat.

In a medium mixing bowl, combine cream of mushroom soup, onion, milk with salt and pepper to taste.

Alternate layer of potatoes, soup mixture and meat in a 2 quart baking dish.

Bake in preheated oven 1 to 1½ hours until potatoes are tender.

Top with shredded cheese.

Shirley McConico

Macaroni Casserole

You'll Need...

1 small package macaroni
¼ c bell pepper, chopped finely
¼ c pimentos, chopped
1large onion, chopped finely
1c mayonnaise
1 c cream of mushroom soup
1 lb. grated cheese

Directions

Cook macaroni drain. Mix all ingredients at 300 degrees for 45 minutes or until bubbles and appearance is light brown.

Asparagus Casserole

You'll Need...

4 eggs (boiled)
(3) 15oz cans asparagus, drained
(2) 10 oz. cans of cream of mushroom soup
2 cups of crushed Ritz crackers
4 oz. of shredded cheese

Directions

Boil eggs then cool and peel and slice.

Preheat oven to 350°.

Grease a 2 quart casserole dish. In a prepared dish layer 1 ½ can of asparagus, 1 can of soup, 2 eggs and 1 cup of crushed crackers.

Repeat layers with remaining ingredients. Cover and bake in preheated oven for 25 minutes.

Remove cover and top with grated cheese.

Cover and bake an additional five minutes or until cheese Is melted.

Shirley McConico

Broccoli Casserole

You'll Need...

2 bags of frozen broccoli
¼ c onion chopped
½ c butter
2 tbsp. flour
1 tbsp. salt
½ c water
8 oz. jar cheese whiz
3 eggs beaten
½ c cracker crumbs

Directions

Set broccoli out to thaw.

Melt butter; add onion, flour, salt, and water.

Stir until smooth.

Add cheese and eggs.

Stir until sauce forms.

Mix ¾ c cracker crumbs and broccoli.

Pour sauce over broccoli.

Sprinkle with remaining cracker crumbs.

Bake at 350° for 45 minutes.

Green Bean Casserole

You'll Need...
2 cans (14oz) French-style green beans (drained)
(1) 10oz. can cream of mushroom soup
¼ c milk
1 can (2.8oz) French-fried onions

Directions
Heat oven to 350°.

Mix green beans, soup, and milk.

Bake 20 to 25 minutes. Topping with during last 5 minutes of baking until bubbly.

Shirley McConico

Squash Casserole

You'll Need...

4 cups sliced squash
½ c chopped onion
1 roll of Ritz crackers
1 cup shredded cheese
2 eggs, beaten
¾ c milk
¼ c butter melted
1 tsp salt, pepper to taste
2 tsps. butter

Directions

Add all ingredients. Preheat over to 400°. Place squash and onion in a large skillet over medium heat. Pour in a small amount of water. Cover and cook until squash is tender, about 5 minutes. Drain well, and place in a large bowl. In a medium bowl, mix together cracker crumbs and cheese.

Stir half of the cracker mixture into the cooked squash and onions. In a small bowl, mix together eggs and milk, then ad to squash mixture. Stir in ¼ cup melted butter and season with salt and pepper. Spread into 9x13 baking dish. Sprinkle remaining cracker mixture and dot with 2 tbsp. butter. Bake in preheated oven for 25 minutes or until lightly browned.

Mom's Corn Casserole

You'll Need...

2½ c whole kernel corn
2½ c tomatoes (stewed)
1 medium bell pepper chopped
1 medium onion chopped
Salt & pepper to taste
1 tbsp. tabasco sauce
1 tsp. sugar
1 c shredded cheese
2 tbsp. melted butter
1½ c cooked rice

Directions

Sauté bell pepper and onions in butter then combine ingredients and place in a greased casserole dish.

Sprinkle with cheese and dot with butter.

Bake in moderate oven, 350°for 40 to SO minutes.

Serves 10.

Shirley McConico

Potato Chip Cookies

You'll Need...

2 sticks of butter softened
½ c sugar
1 tsp. vanilla
1¾ c self-rising flour
½ c crushed thin potato chips
½ c chopped pecans

Directions

Mix in that order, roll in balls, put on ungreased cookie sheet, and flatten with fork.

Bake at 350 for 12-14 minutes.

Coconut Pie

You'll Need...

1 stick butter
1½ c sugar
½ c buttermilk
3 eggs
1 tsp vanilla flavor
1 can coconut
1 unbaked pie crust

Directions

Mix all ingredients and pour into an unbaked pie shell.

Bake at 300° for about 45 minutes or until done.

Bread Pudding

You'll Need...

1 loaf of French bread
1 qtr. whole milk
3 eggs
1 ½ c of sugar
2 tbsp. vanilla flavor
½ c of raisins
3 tbsp. Butter, melted
½ can apples (drained)
Cinnamon to taste

Directions

Preheat oven to 350°.

For pudding, break bread into small pieces. Pour milk in a small bowl and soak bread.

Sprinkle apples with cinnamon, stir and then add to bread mixture.

Mix together eggs, sugar, vanilla, butter and raisins, add to bread mixture and stir.

Pour mixture into a greased 9x13 pan and bake for 45 minutes or until firm. Serve with sauce.

For sauce: combine sugar and butter in double boiler and cook until well dissolved. Add well-beaten egg mix with hand mixer. Cook until thickened.

Sweet Potato Pudding

You'll Need...

3 to 4 large sweet potatoes
2 c sugar
3eggs
2 sticks of butter
2 tsp vanilla flavor
1 tsp lemon flavor
½ c carnation milk

Directions

Cut potatoes in cubes and boil until tender, drained into a large mixing bowl and add ingredients.

Mix until creamy then pour into a 9x13 Pyrex dish.

Bake for 45 minutes on 350° or until done.

Strawberry Sour Cream Pie

You'll Need...
1 deep dish (unbaked) pie crust
1 quart strawberries washed & halved
le plain flour
1/8 tsp salt 8oz sour cream

Directions
Preheat oven to 450°

Place sliced strawberries in bottom of pie crust.

Sift flour, sugar and salt.

Pour in bowl and stir in sour cream.

Mix well and spread over strawberries.

Bake 10 minutes at 450° then 30 minutes at 350°.

Refrigerate before serving.

Butternut Cake

You'll Need...

1 cup of butter or Crisco
2 cups of sugar
3 cups of (White lily) plain flour sifted
3 tsp. baking powder
4 eggs
2 tsp of vanilla extract
1 cup of whole milk or carnation

Directions

Cream butter, sugar then add eggs one at a time.

Then add one cup of flour at a time.

Add milk and vanilla extract.

Mix until consistency is smooth.

Preheat oven at 350°. Pour mixture into 3 9" cake pans greased and floured to avoid cake sticking to the pan. Bake for 40 minutes at 350° or until done.

Place layers onto a cooling rack.

Butternut Cake Frosting

You'll Need...

½ c pecans chopped
sugar
½ butter
½ c walnuts
1 ½ tsp vanilla
3 egg yolks
½ carnation milk

Directions

Add sugar butter then egg yolks and milk.

Cook in a double boiler on a very low heat.

Stir until mixture begins to thicken then add chopped nuts.

Cook until thick enough to spread onto cakes.

Let frosting cool before spreading onto cake.

Shirley McConico

Pound Cake

You'll Need...

1 ¾ c Crisco (May use Crisco and ¾ c butter)

eggs

3 c sugar

3 ½ c of cake flour

1 c buttermilk

1 tbsp. vanilla

DIRECTIONS

Cream Crisco and sugar.

Add eggs one at a time, then add vanilla.

Next add flour and milk alternating.

Mix well.

Bake 1½ hours at 350°

Chocolate Pie

You'll Need...

1 ¼ c of cold milk
2 boxes of choc pudding mix (4oz box)
(1) 9oz cool whip
1 graham cracker crust (large)

Directions

Mix milk and pudding mix for one minute.
Whisk in half of cool whip.
Carefully spread In crust.
Spread the remaining of cool whip over top.
Refrigerate until ready to serve.

Orange Delight

You'll Need...

1 large Jell-O
(1) 20 oz. can crushed pineapple (drained)
1 lrg. can fruit cocktail (drained)
½ c chopped pecans
1 tbsp. sour cream
1 lrg. cool whip

Directions

Mix pineapple and fruit cocktail into a large bowl.

Add Jell-O, pecans, and sour cream.

Then stir cool whip until its smooth and your desired color.

Refrigerate.

Banana Pudding

You'll Need

¾ c sugar
1/3 c all-purpose flour
1 dash salt
4 egg yolks
2 c carnation milk
½ tsp. vanilla extract
1 box of vanilla wafers (reserve 10 to garnish)
4 medium ripe bananas

Directions

Combine ½ cup sugar, flour, and salt in top of double boiler.

Stir flour, egg yolks, and blend well. Cook uncovered over boiling water, stir constantly until thickened.

Reduce heat and cook stirring occasionally, for a few minutes. Remove from heat and add vanilla extract.

Layer a quart casserole dish with wafers and bananas then pour custard over wafers and bananas.

Beat egg whites until stiff but not dry, gradually add the¼ c sugar and beat until peaks form.

Spoon on top of pudding.

Bake at 425 degrees for 3 minutes or until browned. Garnish with remaining wafers.

ACKNOWLEDGEMENTS

I would like to express my very great appreciation to Pastor C. Shaemun Webster for all of the advice, encouragement, and assistance in my writing this book. Your willingness to give your time so generously has been very much appreciated. You have been extremely supportive and helpful throughout this project. Thanks for your patience, time, and support, it has cause me to be a much stronger and confident person and I will forever be grateful. Thanks again!

ABOUT THE AUTHOR

Shirley Cunningham McConico, a woman of poise, purpose, and power, is a testimony that it is never too late to live out your dreams and employ your deepest desires. Shirley is a woman of faith and pursues God with every fiber in her being; never settling and always reaching higher. Throughout life, Shirley has matriculated through challenges, learned lessons along the way that allowed her to develop the motto: "Live Intentionally!"

Shirley's new book, *Your Destiny Has a Diet,* is an innovative, cutting-edge cookbook and devotional all-in-one! *Your Destiny Has a Diet* guides readers through delicious recipe options and encourages the reader to be intentional about their diet with destiny in mind.

Shirley, a native of Alexander City, Alabama, graduated from Benjamin Russell High School. She received a diploma in Data Entry, Computer Operations, and Accounting Clerk from John Patterson Tech College in Montgomery, AL. Shirley also received an Associate Degree in Christian

Leadership from the School of Ministry Excellence of The Tower of Prayer Church in Leeds, AL. Shirley is a servant at heart – serving in many ministries at her church, volunteering in her community, and making a difference in the lives of others. Shirley also loves writing, fishing, shopping, cooking, traveling, and being a vessel of encouragement through social media platforms.

Amongst many other accomplishments, Shirley is a proud mother of three: Kevin, Jonathan and Loretha; three grandchildren, Kia, Kingston and Londyn.

STAY CONNECTED

Thank you for purchasing *Your Destiny Has a Diet*. Shirley would like to connect with you! Below are a few ways you can connect with Shirley for more information about speaking engagements, book releases, book signings, and more!

FACEBOOK Shirley C. McConico
INSTAGRAM @Shirleymc56
WEBSITE www.ShirleyCMcConico.com
EMAIL mcconico39@gmail.com

Made in the USA
Columbia, SC
02 December 2022

72513776R00067